Based on a True Story

MADDIE AND BENJI
Go to School

Written by Stephanie McConnell

Illustrated by KidsBook Art, LLC

Published by

Principal Principles Publications

Ordering Information:
Quantity sales. Special discounts are available on quantity purchases by corporations, associations, and others. For details, contact the publisher at the address above.

Dedication & Thank You

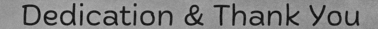

This book is dedicated to all the incredible people who helped bring Benji into Maddie's life. A special thank you to the families who purchased lemonade, and rallied to support and raise money for Benji. Your generosity and dedication made this dream come true. We are deeply grateful to the communities of Hawkins, Pittsburg, and all of East Texas, as well as the local businesses that stood by us every step of the way. A special thank you to Hawkins ISD teachers, nurses, and administration for supporting Maddie!

A heartfelt thank you to Bowen Elite Service Dogs for training Benji and giving Maddie the most wonderful companion and protector she could ever ask for. Finally, to all those fighting the battle of diabetes–you are true warriors. Your strength and perseverance inspire us every day.

This story is for you!

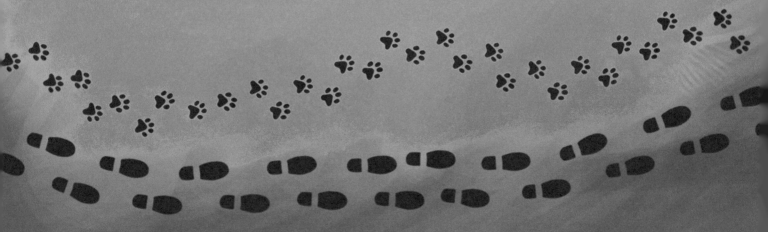

Every day at school was an adventure for Maddie and her best friend, Benji. Maddie was in the first grade, and Benji was her loyal service dog. Benji had a special job–he helped Maddie manage her Type 1 Diabetes.

In the classroom, Benji had his own cozy spot right next to Maddie's desk. All the kids in the class thought Benji was amazing, but they knew he wasn't just any dog. Benji could tell when Maddie's sugar levels were too high or too low, even before Maddie knew.

Mrs. Honeycutt, the teacher, explained to the class, "Benji is here to help Maddie stay healthy. When Maddie's sugar levels go too high or too low, Benji will let her know by gently pawing at her. If you see Benji do this, it's his way of saying, 'Maddie, check your sugar levels!'"

One day, while the class was working on a craft project, Benji started to gently paw at Maddie's leg. Maddie understood right away–Benji was telling her that something wasn't right. She took out her special meter and checked her sugar levels.

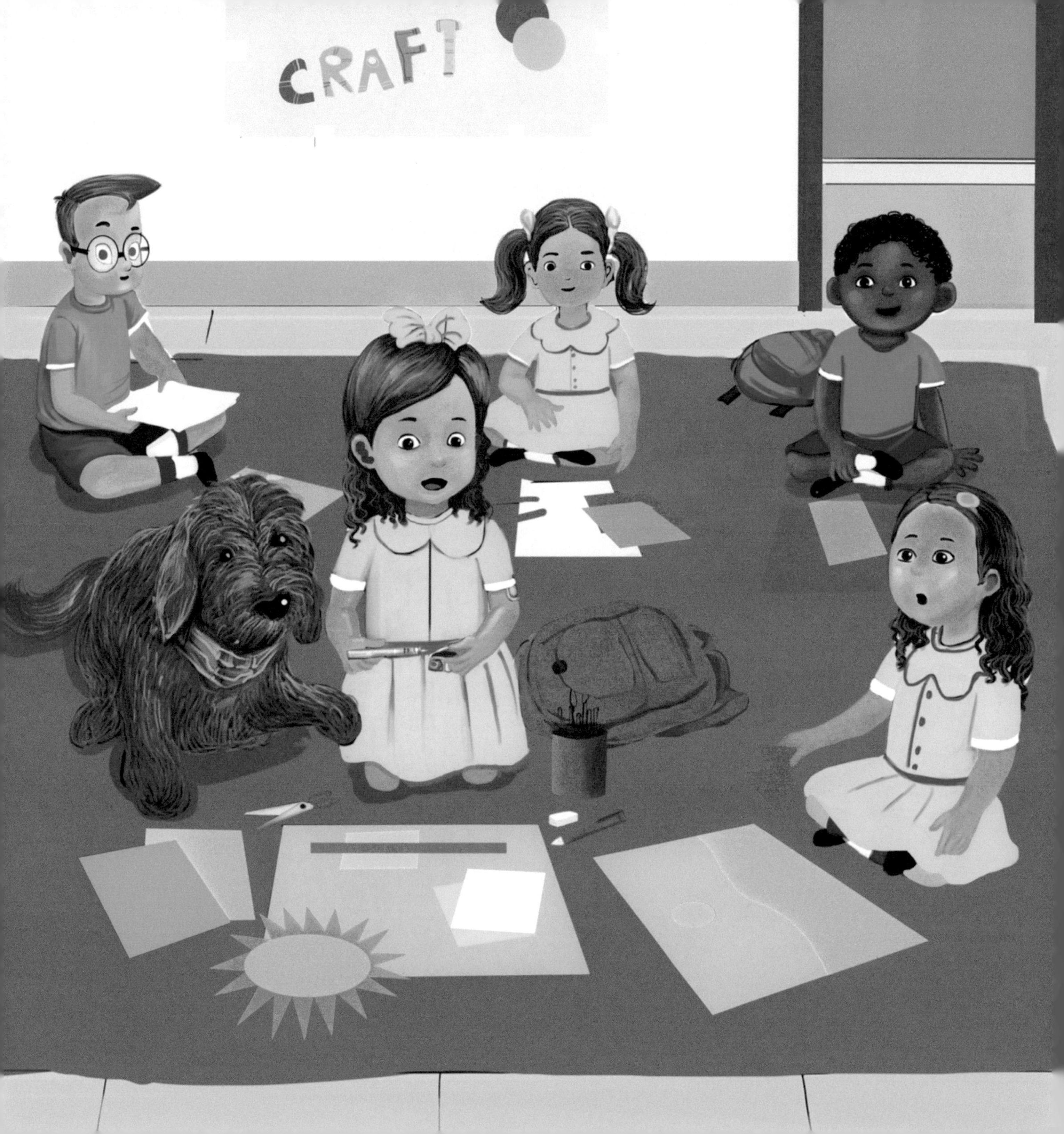
CRAFT

"Oh no," Maddie thought. "My sugar levels are low." Maddie felt her hands start to tremble, and she noticed how tired and shaky she was beginning to feel. Her head felt a little fuzzy, too. She quickly ate a snack from her lunchbox, and Benji sat down, wagging his tail happily.

He knew Maddie was going to be just fine now, and soon Maddie could feel her energy returning as the snack started to work.

Benji wasn't just a helper. He was part of the classroom too!

During story time, he would curl up by Maddie's feet, listening to the stories with the rest of the class. And during recess, he would watch over Maddie, making sure she was safe and having fun.

But Benji had an important job, so even though everyone wanted to pet him, Mrs. Honeycutt reminded the class, "Benji is here to work, so we need to let him focus on helping Maddie. You can say hello, but no petting–he has a very important job to do."

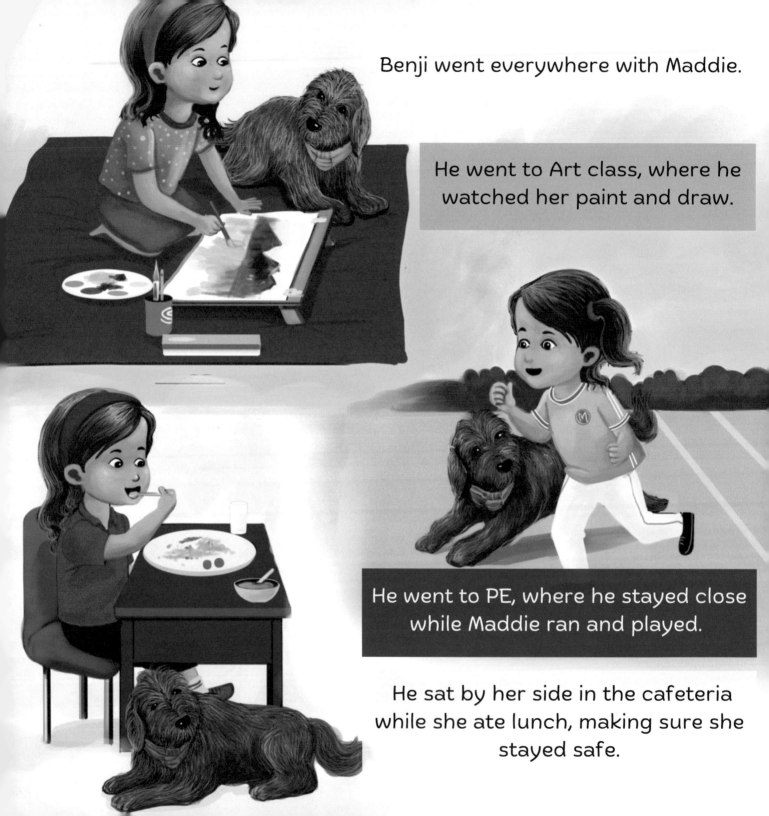

Benji went everywhere with Maddie.

He went to Art class, where he watched her paint and draw.

He went to PE, where he stayed close while Maddie ran and played.

He sat by her side in the cafeteria while she ate lunch, making sure she stayed safe.

Benji was with Maddie during Reading, Math, and Science too. He would lay quietly beside her as she learned new things, always ready to help if she needed him. Wherever Maddie went, Benji went too, making sure she was never alone.

The other kids learned that Benji was more than just a cute dog. He was Maddie's protector and best friend. They knew that having Benji in the classroom was special because it meant Maddie could stay safe and be just like everyone else.

At the end of each day, Maddie gave Benji a big hug. "Thank you, Benji," she whispered. Benji wagged his tail and licked her cheek, letting her know he would always be there to help her every single day at school.

And so, Maddie and Benji went to school together every day. With Benji by her side, Maddie knew she could do anything because Benji was not just a dog—he was her hero.

As they walked home, Maddie smiled and thought about all the fun they had in class. She knew that with Benji by her side, she was never alone. Benji was part of the school family now, and everyone loved him as much as Maddie did.

DID YOU KNOW?

Did you know that service dogs like Benji are real heroes in schools and homes all around the world? They help people with special medical needs, just like Maddie, by detecting changes in their bodies that even people can't feel right away. Service dogs are trained from a young age to use their incredible sense of smell to tell when someone's sugar levels are too high or too low. When they sense something is wrong, they alert their person by pawing, nudging, or even barking. This amazing ability helps keep their person safe and healthy every single day. Benji might be a character in this story, but the work he does is very real, and it makes a big difference in people's lives.

In the summer of 2023, **Jarrod, Ashley and their daughter Maddie Bockmon,** spent every weekend running lemonade stands with a heartfelt mission: **raising money for Benji, Maddie's diabetes service dog.** Benji will help Maddie by detecting dangerous changes in her blood sugar levels, offering us extra support and peace of mind. Through this experience, we not only worked to make this dream a reality but also found a powerful way to raise awareness about Type 1 Diabetes (T1D).

Type 1 Diabetes is an autoimmune condition where the pancreas no longer produces insulin, a hormone necessary for blood sugar regulation. People with T1D require insulin therapy, constant monitoring of blood sugar levels, and careful management to prevent complications. It affects people of all ages, often starting in childhood, and it can be overwhelming for families like ours.

Our hope through these efforts, and now with the Maddie & Benji series, is to shine a light on what life with T1D looks like, sharing not only the challenges but also the resilience, strength, and support needed. We want to provide other families living with T1D a sense of community and understanding, while educating others about this condition.

If you'd like to learn more about Type 1 Diabetes or support ongoing research, here are some resources:

- **Breakthrough T1D (formerly known as JDRF): www.breakthrought1d.com**
- **Beyond Type 1: www.beyondtype1.org**
- **American Diabetes Association (ADA): www.diabetes.org**
- **Follow her journey and more: www.facebook.com/903T1D**

Together, we can spread awareness and support those affected by T1D.

Made in the USA
Columbia, SC
17 November 2024

46148837R00018

DON'T BE A BURDEN
(Youth Edition)

Don't Be A Burden
Written by: Dr. KK MIDDLETON
PUBLICIST: The EROC Group, LLC

Dedication

Dedicating this book to the members of
Sweet Canaan Missionary Baptist Church of Tuskegee,
B ON U Theological Institute & GRACE CHURCH MGM.

Say thank you when people give you something.

Pick up your toys and put them away once you're finished.

Share with others when they don't have something.

Respect your elders and follow their instructions.

Don't joke on people. Say something nice about everyone.

Don't waste food. Only put on your plate the food you're willing to eat.

Lunchtime Rules.

1. We wash our hands before eating.

2. We line up quietly and talk quietly.

3. We show respect to the staff on duty.

4. We remember to say please and thank you.

5. We use a knife, fork and spoon.

6. We do not talk with our mouth full.

7. We tidy up our mess when we have finished.

Never attack people. If you have an issue, talk about it.

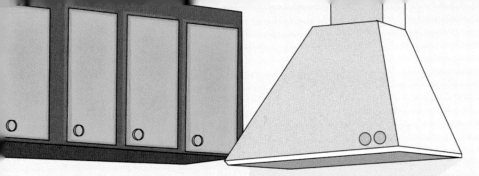

Always wash your hands before eating and after eating.

Never take medicine that your parents didn't get from the doctor or Pharmacy.
(Say NO TO ILLEGAL DRUGS)

Never type hateful things on social media.
Only build people up, never tear them down.

Never join a street gang. Join a book club, a gym and a church where people are nice and not mean.

Always brush your teeth in the morning, noon & night and don't forget mouthwash.

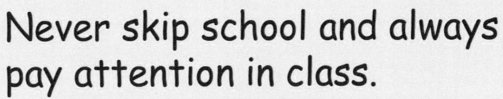

Never skip school and always pay attention in class.

Ask for help when you're in trouble and don't understand.

Always tell the truth.

Smile, it could brighten someone's day.

Save 10 cents out of every dollar.

Bathe daily and wear clean clothes.

The End

Made in the USA
Columbia, SC
20 March 2023

13752170R00015